E.J. Hamilton

Uncle John in the Army and Among the Freedmen

E.J. Hamilton

Uncle John in the Army and Among the Freedmen

ISBN/EAN: 9783743377998

Manufactured in Europe, USA, Canada, Australia, Japa

Cover: Foto ©ninafisch / pixelio.de

Manufactured and distributed by brebook publishing software
(www.brebook.com)

E.J. Hamilton

Uncle John in the Army and Among the Freedmen

AMONG THE FREEDMEN.

PUBLISHED BY THE
AMERICAN TRACT SOCIETY,
150 NASSAU-STREET, NEW YORK.

A sketch of "Uncle John," prepared by Rev. E. J. Hamilton, chaplain in the army of the Potomac, was published in the Appendix of "Toils and Triumphs of Union Missionary Colportage for Twenty-five Years." Its vivid and accurate delineation of the characteristics of this remarkable man, awakened so much interest in those who were familiar with his work, that it has been thought advisable to issue it in the present form. The narrative of his labors since the war on the field of the Richmond Agency of the American Tract Society, is continued to the present time; and a condensed view of the operations of the Society in its efforts to evangelize the South is presented.

JULY, 1867.

UNCLE JOHN.

IN THE ARMY.

IF one should visit the army of the Potomac, and stay for some time in any part of it,
he would be pretty certain to meet an odd
little man going round among the boys. He
generally has a satchel slung over his shoulder, or a package under his arm, or both;
and if you should see him approaching your
home, where scenes are peaceful, you would
prepare for an interview with an old-fashion-
ed, energetic dealer in some kind of small-
wares. His appearance, though not remarkable, excites interest; and you say to yourself, "I wonder what that man is doing in
the army." He is about five feet six inches in
height, and of a square-built, chunky frame;
he wears a soft felt hat and a brown coat, both
of which have done good service; his vest and

pants, a little soiled, suggest that he works actively sometimes; his warm shirt, of gray stocking-web, has been selected for comfort rather than beauty; the paper collar, without any necktie, buttoned carelessly on the shirt, is the only mark about him of any deference to fashion; and the plain, unpolished shoes, which are of the kind that soldiers have, put it beyond denial that the little man is given to walking. His face has a somewhat abstracted expression, yet indicates kind-heartedness, vivacity, humility, and shrewdness. He seems between fifty and sixty years of age; time and care have made furrows on his cheeks, and his dark brown hair is growing thin and sparse. But his eye is bright and restless; and he shoves along with his bundle under his arm, as though he had plenty of business on hand.

Mark him as he enters a camp and is recognized by the soldiers. "Hey, Uncle John, is that you?" says one, who starts to meet him. "How are you, Uncle John?" echoes another from within his tent. "I am glad to see you, Uncle John. Have you any soap

to-day?" cries a third; and a fourth nephew
inquires, "Uncle John, have you brought the
writing-paper and envelopes you promised?"
The wide-awake, earnest man is at home among
them, and answers in a cheery, lively way,
"How are you, dear boys? I'm glad to see
you. I guess I've got a little something for
you—I was thinking you'd be wanting a
little paper and needles, for the paymaster
has n't been round for a good while, has he?
Just step up, boys; I can't carry much, you
know, but I'll give you what I've got." He
is instantly surrounded by a circle of our
blue-coated heroes, ready for his little gifts,
and yet more ready for what Uncle John may
have to say; for they know well that he
never finds himself among soldiers without
saying something that is worth listening to.

Hark to the merry laughter, as Uncle John
makes some singular observation! See the
fixed attention, as he relates some stirring
news, or interesting incident! Listen to
"That's so, Uncle John; that's so," as he
renders some excellent sentiment or advice,
in his terse, striking way! And all the time

both his hands are busy dispensing sheets of
paper, and pens, and thread, etc., with skil-

ful and impartial generosity. After these
gifts, tracts and religious reading are produced from the black satchel, and distributed to many glad recipients, Uncle John
meanwhile continuing his remarks. Now
his stock is exhausted; and he earnestly

repeats an invitation which he has already
given incidentally, perhaps half-a-dozen times.
"Now boys, do n't forget the prayer-meeting
the chaplain is going to have this evening.
Come, come, dear boys, and let us ask God
to bless us." "We will, Uncle John, we
will," is the response of many voices; and
possibly the evening hour will show that the
invitation has been also accepted by many
silent, softened hearts that did not dare to
speak. The next moment "Uncle Johnnie's
gone," but the influences of his genial soul
are scattered all around.

The full name of this ubiquitous wide-awake
man, who has all the soldiers in the army of
the Potomac for his nephews, is known to but
few of those who are familiar with his coun-
tenance and person; but it is a name which
is enrolled for everlasting life and honor in
the blessed book above. He labors as distributing agent for the Sanitary Commission,
and as army colporteur of the American
Tract Society, by whom he is supported; but
he is so original a genius, and such an active,
whole-souled, liberal-hearted philanthropist,

that it is difficult to think of him as connected with any particular institution. I was
struck with the remark of a colored man, as
some were discussing the character of Uncle
John : "I'll just tell you, then, what I thinks;
I thinks this—I thinks Uncle John is a *real
Christianity.*" The truth could scarcely be
expressed better. While entertaining decided
denominational sentiments and attachments,
Uncle John labors everywhere with such a
largeness of spirit, and such a loftiness of
view, that one can regard him only as be-
longing to the church of God and the religion
of Jesus Christ.

The first half of his life was passed in his
cousin's brewery, and was thoroughly given
to business; but about fifteen years ago God
touched the brewer's heart, and claimed him
for a higher service. A severe struggle with
old views and habits terminated in complete
triumph, and he consecrated to the cause of
Christ those energies which had been devoted to secular concerns. Uncle John aban-
doned his position in the brewery, and with
it flattering prospects of wealth. He felt that

it could be his calling no longer. "Heaven," I have heard him say, "seemed too far away when I looked up at it from among the beer barrels." Disengaged from worldly pursuits, he gave himself with zeal to tract distribution, exhortation, prayer-meetings, and various evangelical labors, so that the good people of P—— were astonished; many even thought him crazed. They did not understand the case. A mind of natural strength and fervency had received a strange and powerful impulse from new-born faith and love. To him, religious things, no longer invisible and distant, were seen and present. His awakened soul accepted Bible truths as living and wonderful realities. Christ's cross and judgment-seat seemed very near, radiant with tender attractions and with awful glories. The curtain concealing futurity had fallen; and from beholding the endless destinies of the righteous and the wicked, he turned to his fellow-men, and earnestly besought them to seek the divine favor and preparation for heaven.

This practical zeal for God and souls, arising partly from natural character and yet more from vivid realization of the truths of religion, was no temporary flame. Burning to-day with its original brightness, and with more than its original fervor, it is the immediate source of the ceaseless Christian activity of our beloved Uncle John. He found but a limited sphere of usefulness in P——, and possibly had cause to feel that it was "his own country." Going westward, he spent some years traversing the prairies of Illinois with horse and wagon, as colporteur of the American Tract Society. God went with him over those grassy solitudes, and blessed his labors, and filled him with joy and praise. It was in this service that he gained that experimental familiarity with the best thoughts of Christian authors, and that wonderful command of religious language which have compensated in great measure for the want of a liberal education, and which have contributed greatly to his success in the work of the Lord.

Returning to P——, he began visiting the churches as Providence opened the door, and became instrumental of untold good in several wide-spread revivals. He went from place to place, "feeling his way," and working with the pastors. P—— county especially thrice witnessed a great outpouring of the Divine Spirit, chiefly in blessing upon his efforts. Finding an interest in some members of a decayed backslidden church, he would spend the day visiting in the congregation from house to house, conversing and praying with every one, and in the evening he would attend a prayer-meeting at the residence of some pious family; "for," says he, "it would never do to commence in a cold church; but after God pours down his Spirit in answer to prayer, then the lecture-room will be needed, and the church too." In those times his soul overflowed with happiness, when sanctuaries were nightly crowded with inquirers, and God came down in love and power, and many souls were saved.

As one of the almoners of the royal bounty of the Sanitary Commission, Uncle John is indefatigable. It is his special delight to find unseen and neglected spots, and to secure for

them their share of comforts. Thousands of
poor fellows bless him for timely and thoughtful care. Indeed, I never met any one who
combined in a similar degree prompt and ex-
act attention to items of business with unre-
mitting spiritual aims and efforts. It seems
part of his religion to neglect nothing. Those
evangelical labors, however, to which his
other pursuits are subsidiary, are the chief
exponents of his character and power. In
these—I can express myself in no other way—
in these Uncle John is *great.* His pleading,
particularizing prayers ; his varied, choice,
and ready store of hymns; his rapid, yet un-
offending directness of personal appeal ; his
easy and quick command of thought and language ; his homely, pointed, and solemn
method in public address ; and his very
appearance, and voice, and manner, unpre-
tending and deferential, yet as earnest and
sympathetic as they possibly could be—all
qualify him to succeed anywhere, but especially with soldiers.

I have been amazed sometimes at the
beauty of his prayers. On one occasion, dur-

ing the heats of summer, we rode together through the woods to a distant pasture, that our horses, then fed only on grain, might enjoy grazing for an hour. Uncle John had been somewhat depressed, and we sat under the shade of a little tree. Suddenly he exclaimed, " Brother H——, let us pray," threw himself forward upon the grass, and instantly began, " O God, on this beautiful day, amid these old woods, and beneath thine own clear heavens, we lift up our souls to thee." His voice, at first slow and full, was rich with melody and pathos; and as petition after petition, exquisitely expressed, followed each other in beautiful succession, I thought the sacred eloquence of that unstudied prayer such as I had never heard before. While the prostrate body rested on hands and knees, crouching in lowliest humility, and the face, with close shut eyes and intensity of expression, sometimes almost touched the ground, the longing, believing spirit seemed to rise, as on angels' wings, into the presence and glory of its God. While we were returning, he said that he seemed to have had a glimpse

of heaven, and was refreshed and comforted.
I could easily believe it.

Uncle John is a great power in a soldier's
prayer-meeting, for he generally imparts to
his fellow-worshippers much of his own spirit.
With excellent wisdom, he invariably looks
to the chaplain for the organization and con-
trol of religious assemblies, even of those in
which he himself may be the principal actor;
"for," he says, "*I'm* nothing but an old shep-
herd dog, and I try to help the pastors in
tending their flocks." But after the meeting
has been set a-going, Uncle John, "assisted,"
as he would say, "by the good Spirit of the
Lord," is the very life of it.

The first time I ever saw him was last winter, near B——, in a chaplain's meeting in
the log church of the brigade. The quaint
sprightliness, the overflowing brotherly love,
the humility and Christian readiness of the
good man, were apparent. Ever since the
completion of the log chapel in our brigade,
an increasing interest in religion had been
manifested among the boys, and Uncle John
promised to attend one of our meetings. He

came, and moved us all by his earnest words and fervent prayers. After this I was going away for ten days, and asked him to look after my boys in my absence. He consented at once. On my return I was prepared for something of a revival, but not to learn that the chapel was crowded, and that meetings were kept up three times a day. · And when I entered the chapel that afternoon, what a scene presented itself! · The place was half Babel, half Bochim. Such a murmuring of confused sounds never before had greeted my ears. Most of the soldiers were kneeling by the benches, several were engaged in prayer, and sobbings and groanings, loud responses, and fervent ejaculatory petitions, resounded in every part of the building. Uncle John was in the midst of the congregation, kneeling in the aisle in front of the pulpit, and seemingly the most engaged of all.

After the principal prayer was over, he rose, and in his sweet tenor voice began a favorite hymn; all joined; and the swelling praise went up through the white trembling canvas roof. Other prayers were offered,

interspersed with verses of hymns and with
remarks by Uncle John and the chaplain;
and before the meeting was dismissed, all
present were earnestly invited to attend the
evening service. It seems that he had insti-
tuted the morning assembly for inquirers and
young converts, and that in the afternoon for
the prayers and exhortations of Christians
generally, while more formal exercises occupied the meeting at night. The excitement
and confusion at first seemed to me excessive
and injurious; but I found that they were to
a certain extent the natural consequences of
religious feeling among the soldiers, and that
they were rather checked than stimulated by
Uncle John; for our soldiers sometimes re-
mind one of those ancient warriors—"*homi-
nes rustici atque militares*"—whom Cicero
mentions as having given vent to their enthu-
siasm in loud shouting. Besides, the other
chaplains did not find the noise objection-
able. The evening meeting was the most
important. Generally there was regular service, including a sermon by one of the chaplains, after which those who loved the Lord

and those who desired to do so, were request-
ed to remain. Commonly very few went
away; and then Uncle John's work began.
After some prayers and hymns, he would
make a short address, and conclude by asking those who felt themselves in need of salvation, and who desired Christians to pray
for them, to stand up. And then what earnestness in persuading sinners to declare for
Christ. He would continue making his remarks, and looking over the assembly, perhaps for a minute, till some one rose, "There's
one," says Uncle John with visible emotion.
"Oh, bless the Lord! There is joy in heaven
over one sinner that repenteth." Then, after
a short pause, he would add in the most inviting tones, "And is there no other precious
soul here that wants a Saviour? Yes, there's
another. God bless you, dear brother. Oh,
it was for such that Jesus died—*Jesus* the
Son of God!" and Uncle John would sing:

"He died for you,
He died for me,
He died to set poor sinners free.
Oh, who's like Jesus,
That died on the tree?"

Another pause. "And is n't there any more who want to love this blessed Saviour? Yes, I see you, dear brother. I knew there would be more. I feel that God is here to-night. And there's another, and another, and another. Oh, hallelujah! Praise the Lord!" Another pause. "Now come, dear friends; do n't be afraid. The Lord is waiting; and Oh, he is waiting to be gracious. You do n't suppose you're too great sinners to be saved, do you? The blood of Jesus Christ cleanseth from all sin. Yes, precious Saviour, precious Saviour, thy blood could cleanse a universe from guilt." In this way he would go on till perhaps a dozen or twenty had risen; after which, in order to intensify good resolutions, he would invite them to the front seats, which were vacated for them. This he did often, not always. After more prayers and hymns, the audience were dismissed, only the inquirers remaining; and then Uncle John and the chaplains conversed and prayed with each individual according to his case.

"Talking meetings," designed chiefly for remarks, exhortations, and relations of personal experience, sometimes took the place of these that I have described; they proved very useful. Uncle John participated in them, as he did in all the rest. The revival interest continued with little abatement for five or six weeks, and resulted in the establishment of small congregations of believers in those regiments that had chaplains. Nearly one hundred and fifty—about one-tenth of the whole brigade—professed faith in Christ, either renewedly or for the first time. Very few of these dear boys are with us now; many are in soldiers' graves; many are sick or wounded at home; some are in southern prisons; and some have finished their term and been discharged. But so far as I know, the great majority have shown that their profession was well-founded.

In all our meetings, Uncle John's singing did excellent service. To use an expression of his own, he is "a walking hymn-book." He has a large variety of hymns at command, set to appropriate tunes, and a wonderful faculty of instantly producing in a meeting the verses and notes specially suitable to

each particular conjuncture. How often have
I heard him, so soon as a prayer or address
might end, strike up the hymn needed to correct or to carry out the impression of it. He
would seldom sing the whole hymn; but if
one or two verses satisfied the occasion, he
would cease, that the meeting might go on.
This tact often helped to render the interest
of our exercises continuous and progressive.

Uncle John's voice is not strong, but it is
clear and pleasant; and as he sings with earnestness and truthfulness of expression, his
lips sometimes seem to clothe old verses with
new beauty, and to impart a striking and
unexpected fulness of meaning to words that
have long been familiar. Those who have
heard him will not forget with what joyous
faith he sings,

> "Jesus shall reign where'er the sun
> Does his successive journeys run ;"

nor how invitingly and solemnly he renders

> "There is a fountain filled with blood,
> Drawn from Immanuel's veins ;"

nor the tenderness of those lines,

> "Come, trembling sinner, in whose breast
> A thousand thoughts revolve ;
> Come with your guilt and fear opprest,
> And make this last resolve ;"

nor the heartiness of the verses,

> "Come, ye sinners, poor and needy,
> Weak and wounded, sick and sore ;
> Jesus ready stands to save you,
> Full of pity, love, and power."

How boldly he raises that Christian battle-song,

> "Am I a soldier of the cross?"

What thankfulness and love he puts into that grand hymn,

> "Oh for a thousand tongues to sing
> My dear Redeemer's praise!"

With what plaintive melody he sings,

> "Did Christ o'er sinners weep?
> And shall my tears be dry?"

and with what affectionate longing,

> "Jerusalem, my happy home."

These and many other old hymns, and the tunes which accompany them, are weapons of power with Uncle John. Besides these, he has a collection of modern religious melodies, generally lively in character, and very popular with soldiers. Those beginning, "My heavenly home is bright and fair;" "There's a light in the window for thee, brother;" "Must Jesus bear the cross alone?" "A beautiful land by faith I see;" and those which tell of the "Sweet hour of prayer," and of "The gospel ship," which is "sailing, sailing," and of "The heavenly shores," to which we are "homeward bound," are fair examples. They commonly have a chorus, which adds to their effect.

I shall not soon forget the delight with which I first heard him singing a song, whose lively notes and cheerful rejoicing confidence accorded admirably with his own spirit. It was towards the close of a crowded meeting in the log-chapel. He rose after a prayer, and turned round in the aisle so as to face the congregation. His right hand held the left by two fingers, and kept it out of the way behind his back. Standing in his humble but easy manner, he began in a clear voice,

"We are joyously voyaging over the main,
Bound for the evergreen shore,
Whose inhabitants never of sickness complain,
And never see death any more."

Warming as he went on, he kept looking over the audience to observe their feeling; and before he had finished, he was clapping his hands quietly in time to the tune, and leading us all in the chorus, like an enthusiastic singing-teacher. The hymn, though familiar now, was then new to most of us, but we could not help joining with Uncle John to the best of our ability in the chorus,

> "Then let the hurricane roar,
>   It will the sooner be o'er ;
>   We will weather the blast, and we'll land at last
>   Safe on the evergreen shore."

Few, perhaps none, went away from the meeting that night without resolving to secure transportation in that good ship, for which, according to his wont, Uncle John was looking up passengers.

Some striking qualities of Brother V——'s character are exhibited in his dealings with others relative to their religious state and duty. His earnestness of manner, his unfeigned and affectionate interest in one's personal welfare, and his entire freedom from any sort of conventionality or constraint,

soon make the heart trustful, and beget open-
ness of conference and confession. During
a time of religious awakening, he labors with
inquirers night and day. At B——, all who
witnessed his zeal marvelled that flesh and
blood could endure such incessant excitement and activity. Three meetings a day, in
all of which he prayed and spoke and sang,
seemed in no degree to diminish his energy
for special and private exertions. For weeks
he spent his spare time in going from tent to
tent conversing and praying with every one
who manifested any concern regarding religion. As he set out one morning to follow
up the impressions of the preceding night, I
went with him down into the company streets.
Entering a tent where two out of the four
occupants were Christians, he addressed himself to each man in suitable inquiries and
exhortations, and led in a short prayer. Then
he asked for a sergeant whom he knew to be
under deep conviction. The young man came
in as we were going out to find him. Uncle
John instantly read the trouble of his face,
which expressed the most profound melan-

choly; and laying his hand affectionately on the shoulder of the young man, exclaimed with sadness and tenderness, "O Albert, Albert, my dear boy, have n't you given your heart to the Saviour yet? What *is* the matter, Albert? Why do n't you throw every thing else away, and trust only in the Lord Jesus?" The young man answered that he was trying to do that, but could not find any

peace. Every thing seemed dark, somehow.
Uncle John replied, " Then you must pray
to God to make it light. *He* can cause light
to shine in darkness. And now, dear boys,
let us all pray for Albert, for nobody but
God can help him, and let Albert pray for
himself. Chaplain, lead us in prayer." We
all knelt down in the little shanty, which
barely held us. The chaplain prayed, and
then Uncle John said, "Now, Albert, *you*
pray." The lad offered a few simple and earnest petitions. We left him with some words
of encouragement. Several days afterwards
I met him going to one of the meetings with
a shining and happy face. " Well, Albert,"
said I, "how do you feel to-day?" "Oh,
bright as a shilling," was the singular but
expressive reply; and bright ever since has
been his Christian character and course.

Uncle John, without being exactly abrupt,
is wonderfully quick and direct in personal
appeal. His preparatory remarks, if he makes
any, are very short; sometimes merely the
manner and evident spirit of the man intro-
duce what he says; but, in any case, the first

startling sentence clears the way for any that may follow. "Here," said I, as we went down the street, "is Sergeant M——, Uncle John." "How are you, sergeant?" says the ever-ready man, taking the sergeant by the hand. "And I hope, chaplain, this good soldier has enlisted under the banner of King Jesus? Dear sergeant, how is it? Now just tell Uncle John. Are you trying to be a faithful servant of God? Have you given yourself to that blessed Saviour who died for you, and who bought you with his precious blood?" As these words were uttered with great earnestness and affection, the sergeant looked thoughtful. He confessed that he was not a Christian, but said that he often desired to be one. "Oh, why then delay? Why risk your eternity? Who knows how soon the whizzing bullet or bursting shell may lay one low? And then, to enter God's presence unprepared! Oh, sergeant, will you not seek the Lord now, and secure that glorious hope which is full of immortality?" With such words, spoken by the way, Uncle John has moved many to seek Christ.

The treatment given to his approaches and exhortations by different parties is very various; but he is equal to any emergency. He instantly appreciates the nature of each case, and gives the instruction, encouragement, reproof, or reply which is needed. I have been astounded sometimes to hear officers, of whose profanity, drunkenness, gambling, and dishonesty, I was well aware, and who never to my knowledge showed even decent respect for religion, tell Uncle John that they were Christian men. I suppose they meant that they had been church-members while in civil life. They seldom deceived him. His interviews with such miserable men are generally made brief. Without even insinuating distrust, he utters a few awakening words, and is gone. "Oh," I have heard him say, "how solemn a thing it is to be called by the name of QHRIST. What a responsibility lies on us to adorn the doctrine of God our Saviour in all things; and how hard it is to be a Christian in *reality*, in deed as well as in name. Yes, dear friends, we must *strive* to enter in at the strait gate. I often think what a mercy it will be if Uncle John ever gets to heaven. It will be by the triumph of grace divine. Oh, the riches of the grace of God!" With such sayings he leaves the backsliders thinking and ill at ease. Consistent believers, on the contrary, seldom meet him without enjoying some bright view of heavenly things, by which their hearts are strengthened in faith and hope and love.

The skill and spirit with which he replies to the pretences of unbelief and to the excuses of the unconverted, could not be surpassed. While maintaining the best temper, and exhibiting overflowing kindness and affection for souls, he attacks every form of sinfulness and error with unsparing fidelity. "O dear captain," I heard him say, "how I wish you would make up your mind to give yourself to the Lord Jesus Christ, and to become a faithful soldier of the cross." "Well, Uncle John," said the captain, "I try to do my duty, and I think that is all that is required of me." "Why, captain," answered the honest man in tones of astonishment, "how *can* you say so? No man does his duty who

does not give his heart to God, and live in
God's love and service.   What would you
think of a man brought up by a kind father,
and provided by him with every means of
happiness, who should be a good brother
and husband and neighbor and citizen, and
yet be a heartless and undutiful son?   Don't
you think his wickedness would be unspeak-
ably great?"   "But the cases are different,"
rejoins the captain.   "No, they 're not," said
Uncle John.   "That man would be condemned by the moral sense of the community; and the godless sinner, you may *depend*
upon it, will be condemned by the public
opinion of the universe."   Thus boldly does
this humble servant of God contend with the
adversary, and assert the prerogatives of his
Master; and he is as ready to do this with
officers in high command as he is with private soldiers.   Colonels and generals have
received faithful admonition from him on
things vital to their eternal peace.

On one occasion, I cannot say whether I
was more amused to see the familiar yet
respectful assurance, or gratified to witness

the startling directness with which he inter-
rogated a brave colonel whom he had never
seen before. A meeting had been concluded
in front of the headquarters' tent, and Uncle
John had conversed and prayed with a young
man who had shown deep conviction and
anxiety regarding his sins. Utterly uncon-
scious of human presence, and with a sim-
plicity and earnestness which rose above all
influences of time and place, and surrounded
themselves with their own proprieties —
silence, solemnity, and attention—he knelt
with the lad in the midst of a crowd of by-
standers, and prayed for him, for his com-
rades, for the officers of the regiment, and
for the whole army. The vigorous colloquial
language of the prayer, and its particularizing petitions, in which names and places
and circumstances were freely mentioned,
interested and impressed the hearers of it.
Conventionalities plainly had little to do with
Uncle John's religion. The young man went
away comforted, and trusting in God; and
the crowd dispersed. Then we entered the
colonel's tent, in which we found one or two

officers of the command, together with their
chief. After a few words of conversation
regarding the history of the regiment and
its part in the summer's campaign, in which
it had lost heavily, Uncle John remarked that
it was a blessed thing to have a hope that no
bullet or cannon-ball can touch, and a life
indestructible and immortal. Then turning
to the colonel, he said in a confidential and
coaxing way, "And now, colonel, just tell
Uncle John how it is with you. We are all
perishing creatures, and must soon be in
eternity together. Have you, dear colonel,
a good hope in Christ? Can you say that
you *know* that your Redeemer liveth? You'll
pardon Uncle John for asking you; he's a
poor dying old man that loves your soul, and
wants it to be saved." This appeal, made
rapidly, without any apparent premeditation,
and with great tact and tenderness, evidently
affected the colonel. Uncle John proceeded
in the same manner as before: "You know
what I mean. I don't mean, Are you a pro-
fessor of religion? for there are many unwor-
thy professors; but, has your heart been re-

newed by grace divine? That is the point. Have you become a new creature in Christ Jesus? Have you experienced that change of which our Saviour speaks when he declares that a man must be born again before he can see the kingdom of God?" The colonel expressed a hope that he was a Christian; and Brother V—— replied that he rejoiced to hear him say so; that he prayed the Lord to bless him and make him faithful to the end; and that he wished before God that all our leaders were earnest, believing men."

I have not spoken hitherto of Uncle John as a public speaker, because the peculiarities of his character are better illustrated by other topics, and perhaps also from a consciousness of inability to describe correctly his more sustained efforts. During the revival of last winter he frequently moved the audiences in the log chapel with short but thrilling strains of extemporaneous eloquence. Few of those who listened to these addresses regarded them in a rhetorical aspect; criticism is not in the line of soldiers; but all felt his power, and agreed that "he knew how to talk."

Those of us, however, who were accustomed
to notice mental methods, could not but wonder at the man's gifts. For myself, I listened
to passages in his oratory such as, I think,
are seldom heard from either pulpit or ros-
trum. His style at times reminded one of
the more serious and moving utterances of
Gough. But his discourses showed more
argument than is commonly attempted in
those of that interesting lecturer. Thought
after thought was presented and illustrated
with admirable though untaught adherence
to the rules of art. The logical order of the
ideas, their progressive continuity of impulse,
their practical development and application,
were faultless. Homely condensed language,
natural and striking metaphors, unexpected
similes, antitheses, and turns of expression, a
becoming gesticulation, and a voice wonderfully persuasive and rich with sympathetic
feeling, engaged attention, awoke the heart's
best emotions, and excited new interest in
the saving truths of Christianity. The sin-
cere and humble earnestness of the man was
also a chief element of his power. Not a

word was uttered for oratorical effect. Every sentence manifested yearning love for souls, vivid conceptions of eternal things, and a solemn sense of the presence of God. Success too, though confidently looked for, was expected solely through the divine blessing. What wonder was it that such speaking produced results that have been visible ever since? For my part, I doubt not that it was instrumental of everlasting good.

During the early part of last summer he labored in the army of the James, among the colored regiments, and as might be conjectured, was very successful in arousing the lively African soldiers to the duties and attractions of religion. Nowhere were his visits more welcome, or the results of his efforts to lead men to the Saviour more apparent, than among the colored troops. They prepared a place in the pine woods with seats and a stand for speakers, where he often addressed them. From one thousand to fifteen hundred souls were frequently present at these meetings. It was a scene worthy of a painter's skill, when the little man,

in his own tender and telling way, addressed
the gathered hundreds of his sable brethren;
and when he led those assemblies in one of
his stirring hymns, I think that the loud notes
of praise rivalled in spirit and grandeur any
that ever echoed from cathedral roofs.

After a time he was induced to have his
headquarters with us, and to make our divis-
ion the principal field of his labors. In this

way I had the privilege, several times during the summer, of hearing him speak in public. His addresses are invariably extemporaneous. He says that deliberate composition is very difficult and irksome for him; which, indeed, might be inferred from his vivacious and emotional temperament, and his want of literary training. His efforts too, though always interesting to his hearers, are not always of equal power. I was particularly pleased with an address which he made one September evening in the plaza of Fort Davis to a regiment drawn up before him in line. The colonel had directed a notification of the companies for a prayer-meeting which we proposed to have; but the adjutant, thinking, I presume, to do the business thoroughly, ordered out the whole command, as if for dress-parade. Uncle John stood with his hands behind him, leaning against a tree in front of the headquarters, while company after company filed past him, faced to the rear, and dressed into correct position. The men evidently were wondering what was going on; and some of the officers seemed to

think that a joke was being perpetrated on
the chaplains and Uncle John. However, we
were ready for the emergency. A prayer-
meeting was out of the question; so we resolved on some public exercises. After an
introductory address, a hymn, and a prayer,
Uncle John was invited to speak. He began
by expressing his gratitude to the colonel for
that opportunity of addressing the officers
and men of "the dear old Seventh." He
had come expecting only to attend a prayer-
meeting, but was glad to meet so many brave
men. As he looked on the faces before him,
and saw how very few were present of those
whom he had seen last winter, the thought
arose, "Where were those brave boys that
left the old camp at B——?" They are
gone; they lie on the battle-fields of the
Wilderness, and of Spottsylvania, and of the
North Anna, and of Coal Harbor—all along
the way from the Rapidan to Petersburg.
Some are at home in the North, or in hospitals; but how many occupy their long, last
home—a soldier's grave! Scarcely one is
left of the familiar faces. Ah, well did he

remember some of those noble boys that he used to see in the old log chapel, and whom he should see never more on earth. But, blessed be God, he had a bright hope of meeting them in heaven. They were heroes of Christ, and of his cross. Now they have fought their fight, they have finished their course, and they have received their crown. Oh, how he wished that every soldier was a truly Christian man, and prepared for any chance that might befall him. He knew many brave men who were not Christians; but it was always a mystery to him how any man could face death without a hope in that blessed Saviour, who had triumphed over death and the grave. He supposed a sense of duty would do much, but how much better was it to be sure that one's soul has been saved with an eternal salvation. Then the king of terrors is dethroned, and death becomes the gate of heaven. Did you never think, he asked, against what love you offend while you remain unreconciled to God? Oh, it filled all heaven with wonder, when God's glorious Son took on him our salvation, and offered himself for our sins. Never was love like His love. How can you refuse your hearts to that loving, dying Saviour? Surely you will not suffer it to be that Christ should have died for you in vain.

"The Son of God in tears.
  Angels with wonder see;
Be thou astonished, O my soul
  He shed those tears for thee.

"He wept that we might weep;
  Each sin demands a tear.
In heaven alone no sin is found,
  And there's no weeping there.'

Dear soldiers, if I know my own heart, I earnestly desire the welfare of you all. God knows that I love you, and want to see you happy. And when I think of the fatigues and exposures and dangers which soldiers must undergo, Oh, how I wish to have them sustained and comforted by the hopes and consolations of the gospel. I would that every one of you had a sure title to a mansion in the skies. I would that you could all look from these scenes of conflict and suffering and death to that blessed land where there is war no more. Oh, yes; no whistling minie ball, no bursting Parrot shell shall disturb the peaceful inhabitants of that heavenly country. In that land there shall be rest for the weary; pain and grief shall not enter there;

> "No groans shall mingle with the songs
> That warble from immortal tongues."

Now let me say a few words to those of you who are Christians. Dear brethren, you are surrounded by temptations; but strive to live faithfully; hold fast your profession; let no man rob you of your crown. Trust not in yourselves, but in One that is mighty. Keep looking up to Jesus, and you will be conquerors, and more than conquerors, through him that loves you. Recently, by the bedside of a dear corporal that formerly belonged to your regiment, but that now sleeps in Jesus, I felt what truth, what power there is in the religion of Christ. All was peace with him, perfect peace. He knew that he was dying; but he rejoiced in the hope of a better life, in the sure prospect of a glorious immortality. "Oh, let me die the death of the righteous, and let my last end be like his." And as for you, dear friends, who are without Christ, will you not seek an interest in his salvation? Will you not begin to love and serve that Redeemer who can save and bless you for ever? Yes, Jesus is the Saviour that you need.

"None but Jesus,
None but Jesus
Can do helpless sinners good."

Oh, then, do not hesitate. To-morrow may be too late. Who knows how soon the bolt of death may come? Now, while it is called to-day, give your hearts to God, and kneel before him in penitence and prayer. Dear soldiers, I thank you for the kind attention with which you have listened to me. May the Lord bless you all, and bring you to his heavenly kingdom.

Such, as nearly as memory serves me, was the course of thought and style of language employed by Uncle John. But the foregoing sketch can give no adequate idea of the living power with which he spoke. His allusions to the uncertainty of life and the nearness of death had a peculiar significance with those whom he addressed. Several of their number had been instantaneously killed, not long before, on the picket line in front of the fort; and a day or two subsequently to our meeting, one poor lad was struck by a minie ball and died in five minutes, a few paces from the spot where he had listened to Uncle John. The summer's campaign had made us all too much accustomed to these things.

Uncle John's labors during the summer with the sick and wounded of the army were

abundant. He went with the trains and the steamboats laden with the disabled of the great battles, and exerted himself incessantly for the welfare of both body and soul. He considered no service too laborious or too menial to perform for the helpless sufferers. Many owe their lives to him, and by him many have been led into the way of life eternal. The large tents which constitute the hospital wards receive daily visits from him, and any special want of their inmates engages his immediate attention. He is particularly ready to converse and pray with those who are dangerously ill, or who express spiritual anxiety. Every evening also, if duty does not call him elsewhere, he assists a chaplain in conducting short exercises. The wards, to the number of eight or nine, are successively visited, and in each of them two or three verses are sung and a prayer is offered. In these services Uncle John's gift of song is most happily employed. His choice variety of hymns, his tact in selecting verses, and his admirable use of tunes, both old and new, contribute greatly to render this evening worship interesting and profitable. I have noticed, too, that occasionally he gives a line according to a version of his own, no way inferior to the variations of the hymn-books.

Besides these employments at the hospitals, a great part of his time is taken up in visiting the camps, where he distributes religious reading and sanitary comforts, and helps the chaplains at prayer-meetings and public services. These journeyings call into play his powers as a pedestrian, which are most extraordinary. He thinks nothing of a stretch of eight or ten miles; and one hot day of last summer I knew him to walk fifteen miles and back again, with very little appearance of fatigue. Everywhere, and among all classes, he finds a cordial welcome. Many chaplains particularly, and among them the writer of this, feel themselves under profound obligations to him; for we are generally agreed that it would be difficult, perhaps impossible, to find another man in the country so well qualified as he for religious labor among soldiers, at least for that kind of labor which Uncle John performs. And certainly no one could enter upon such work with more self-devoting zeal than that which animates this singularly-gifted man. The camp and hospital, the march and the bivouac, the siege-line and the battle-field, have witnessed his untiring energy in the service of a Divine Master. Ten thousand thanks to the American Tract Society for sustaining such a man in so blessed a work.

When I look upon Uncle John as he is now, a ready and mighty laborer in the cause of man's regeneration, and compare him with what he was sixteen years ago, the lively and driving manager of work in a brewery, I exclaim, "How powerful is the grace of God; what changes it can effect; how marvellously it fashions the most un-likely materials into blessed instrumentali-ties of good!" Under its influence, abilities and habits developed in a life of eager world-liness are employed with singular efficiency in the pursuit of heavenly objects; the want of early preparation and instruction is com-pensated by the improvement of a devoted mind; and a holy consecration of purpose is

unflinchingly sustained for years, and crown-
ed with ever-increasing success. Such an
instance is rare; so that none should presume to squander precious time in the hope
of future faithfulness; but what encouragement it contains for those, of whatever age or
condition of life, who feel themselves called
to some special department of the service of
God. How surely he can sustain and pros-
per us, while in some fitting sphere we labor
earnestly for him!

I now bring to a close my intellectual com-
panionship with Uncle John; and I do so
with regret. It has pleasantly occupied some
evenings, which otherwise might have passed
unimproved in the bomb-proof and the wall-
tent. Fare ye well, dear, good man. You
have sometimes been a sad reproof to me for
my want of resolution and fidelity in the dis-
charge of a holy calling—a reproof none the
less potent because all unconsciously admin-
istered : but for that I bear you no ill-will; I
rather render thanks to Heaven that I have
seen the living power of Christianity brightly
illustrated, and I pray God for a baptism of

his Holy Spirit, that I may more successfully emulate the example of his devoted servants, in closely following the footsteps of our divine Saviour. Fare ye well, dear Uncle John. May God long spare you, a blessing to your kind, and at last take you gently to his heavenly home. And when separating years shall have passed away; when the great war, now nearing its end, shall have been succeeded by times of national prosperity; when your friend the chaplain shall have attained his desire, and be the pastor of some peaceful village flock; when your moving and persuasive voice shall be hushed in death; when your face and form, now welcome and familiar, shall present themselves no more for cordial greetings; and when your triumphant spirit, freed from earth's fetters, shall be rejoicing on high, in the activities of an immortal life—then it may give pleasure to review these pages, the souvenir of the acquaintance of a twelvemonth; to recall lovingly the most cherished memories of one's army life, and to think of a sainted Uncle John.

AMONG THE FREEDMEN.

Such is the record of this faithful, earnest
seeker of souls, as given by Chaplain E. J.
Hamilton, who watched his course as an
army missionary of the American Tract Society in the Army of the Potomac. He was
actively engaged in this work to the close of
the war, ministering to the temporal and
spiritual wants of his beloved soldier-boys
through the terrible battles of the spring of
1865, that resulted in the capture of Petersburg and the evacuation of Richmond.

The active work of campaigning being
over, his heart turned with ardent longing to
relieve the spiritual necessities of the people
that had been so long desolated by the pri-
vations and ravages of war. Over one-third
of the land, schools and colleges had been
broken up, the churches were closed or dis-
mantled, the congregations dispersed and the
pastors gone, and the religious literature that
for years had been accumulating in the fam-

ilies and churches and Sabbath-schools had been scattered or destroyed during the war.

At the anniversary of the Tract Society in May, 1865, the question, How shall the ruin thus wrought be overcome, the schools be regathered, the churches reopened, the pastors recalled, the libraries of ministers and people be supplied with a Christian literature, and all the agencies for evangelization be again set fully to work? pressed with painful weight upon the committee and officers. Realizing that the Society possessed peculiar facilities for an immediate and most beneficent work over the whole South, they proposed the following resolution for the adoption of the meeting:

"*Resolved*, That the desolated South reopens to the missionary colportage of this union Society a field of labor vast and needy; and in Christ's name we will strive, with all good men, to make it a garden of the Lord."

The sentiment of this resolution met a hearty and prompt response, and the way was opened at once for renewing the work which in former years had been so useful, and which seemed now so peculiarly fitted for the emergency.

Immediately after the anniversary, Rev. George L. Shearer was commissioned as District Secretary of the Southern Atlantic states, and with a large supply of books and tracts was sent to Richmond, and authorized to prosecute colporteur operations as the way should be opened. When the plan was proposed to Uncle John Vassar to engage in the work with Mr. Shearer, he replied with characteristic promptness, "I am ready to go; my heart is in Richmond; I long for their souls." He reached that city on Saturday, and the next day entered on the work of winning souls to Christ with all the earnestness of his loving heart.

In his first communication, after giving details of his interesting work, he says, " By the help of God, I would plead for the poor white and colored people of this desolated part of our country, until every Christian and friend of his country shall feel the responsibility God has rolled upon us to help them in this hour of need. What shall be

the character of this population? How may
we labor to stamp the image of Christ on
the hearts of thousands? These are weighty
questions with me. Oh for youthful strength
and heavenly grace to labor for my dearest
Lord."

He has since continued his labors in that
Agency, making repeated visits to various
portions of Virginia, North and South Carolina, ascertaining the necessities of the people, supplying them with books, organizing
day-schools and Sabbath-schools, holding
religious meetings, and laboring with great
zeal in many revivals of religion. While his
tender sympathy is ever quick to respond to,
and as far as possible to relieve, the physical
suffering so general and widespread over his
field, his absorbing concern is for the education of the children and youth, white and
black, and particularly for the conversion of
the souls of all. And in these efforts his
labors have been richly blessed.

Soon after the commencement of the work
in Richmond, he wrote: "I am busy every
day and night among the colored people. A

large number are under conviction, and need constant instruction. I find a good opportunity to reach the children, and labor for their good at the close of their schools. Quite a number of our scholars in our Sunday-school have found Christ, and it is blessed to see their happy faces on Sunday morning as they make their way in haste to school. Hundreds know me, and cry, 'Uncle John, how do you do?' I am getting more and more interested in the children. I have thousands of nephews and nieces, and feel no shame as they recognize me as 'Uncle John.' All I want is to meet these thousands in the house of many mansions. Jesus will have many jewels set in dark caskets to stud his crown.

"The success of the colored schools has awakened the interest of the white churches for the education of the blacks. I am doing what I can to put the Bible and our good books into the hands of the colored children that have learned to read. Some of our meetings are largely attended, as many as a thousand having been present. I am comforted in the assurance that a good religious interest is arising in all the churches. Let prayer be offered continually for this great object. In the widespread influences of the religion of Christ, I see the only great and permanent prosperity of the South.

" The great field among the whites is found on Oregon Hill, a village in the suburbs of the city. A little beyond the village, I passed over a large field of graves, where lay so many of the men of both armies. I thought of the many hopes buried with the bodies of the poor boys sleeping away from friends and home. My heart was touched with the remembrance of the past; but another feeling filled my bosom as I saw crowds of living forms, small and great, passing before me as I entered the city, and to-day I look out upon the thousands I have been mingling with, and feel impelled to lift my heart to heaven for their salvation. Oh that the church of Christ was awake to the interests of these unnumbered souls that are ready to perish in the midst of poverty.

" Such a field as we find in Virginia is seldom looked upon by Christian men. There are thousands of colored people who need to be taught to read and to be led to look to Jesus for salvation. In their unsettled state they need God-fearing men to encourage them religiously, and teach them in temporal matters what is for their good. The Tract Society has already done a work in its colporteur labors that is priceless. While the Freedmen's Bureau is doing much to feed this class of the suffering at the South, the Tract Society is meeting a want that has not been met by any other to any great extent. Thousands of the colored people thank us for our labors and our prayers, and the poorer class of whites receive us gladly when they know our object in coming among them. Could we only have the books and men to reach the different counties of this great state, God only knows the good that might be done."

While laboring in Richmond, the Spirit of God was poured out upon the colored people. He engaged in the work with all the ardor of his soul, devoting his efforts particularly to the First African church, the great church of the colored people, where the work

continued for a long time with deep interest.
At one period almost the entire body of the
church was given up to those inquiring the
way to Jesus. He met the members of the
church in prayer at daybreak, visited and
prayed in the families until noon, conversed
with the children in the schools who were
awakened from 12 to 1 o'clock, met the inquirers with the pastor at 4 p. m., and in his
simple yet direct and effective way addressed
the body of the people at 7 o'clock. Over
three hundred were added to the church as
the result of this revival. His labors here,
and in his frequent visits to other parts of
his field, were very arduous; but his heart
was greatly cheered by the anxiety of the
people to learn, and by the constant eviden-
ces of the Holy Spirit. "Two things," he
says, "keep me from fainting by the way:
the children learn so fast, and many are coming to Christ. Sometimes as many as fifty
have united with the colored churches on a
Sunday. They organize churches in the
woods, and build log-houses to worship God
in, and teach their children to read. Every

visit to the country convinces me that we have the grandest mission field in America."

The desire manifested by the colored people, old and young, for education, which is justly prized by them as the highest boon of their newly-acquired freedom, and which has known no abatement till the present time, affected Uncle John from the very first with peculiar interest. He has not regarded it as a matter of transient importance, but with far-seeing wisdom has discovered in this new-born zeal a solution of the problem that has awakened so much solicitude: What shall be the future of that large class so suddenly introduced into the duties and responsibilities of freemen? Deeply impressed that they are to be the teachers of their own race, if they are to be extensively taught, he has been earnestly at work, under the direction of the District Secretary, in organizing and encouraging schools among the colored people, sending repeated appeals to the North, that the friends of the African should do all in their power to supply them now with the means of education.

While none have been more delighted at the repeated and remarkable instances of progress in the acquirement of knowledge, his rejoicing has not been so much at the evidence of personal improvement, as at the prospect that these scholars were thus preparing to become teachers, and would thus aid in the diffusion of knowledge so essential to the elevation of their race.

"This is the way," he says, "that much of · this great field must be reached. If we have to depend on teachers from the North, and money to support them in every part of the South, we should never see half of the field occupied. We get every colored man and woman to work that can read or spell. They must be encouraged to help one another. Millions of money could not do this work if we have to depend on Northern teachers alone. Several schools have been started to fit young persons to go to the country as soon as possible, and teach their race. We shall have thousands of young colored people to take these little schools in rural districts; and who can tell the results of this wonderful work? A door of usefulness like this has never been opened to the church in our land."

He has also been gratified in noticing the awakening desire on the part of many young men, after becoming interested in their studies, to make preparation for the gospel ministry. This desire he has always encouraged, believing that their people, as they realize the advantages of education, will demand a higher order of preaching than that with which they have been supplied.

Thus is this earnest man indefatigably engaged in the work so dear to his heart, of spreading the gospel in the South, through the instrumentalities placed in his hand by his "good old mother," as he always affectionately styles the American Tract Society, in whose service he has labored for seventeen years. His work has been most fruitful in removing prejudice, in melting down hostility by the ardor of his Christian love, in disseminating widely the privileges of education, and in building up the kingdom of Christ, gathering into it from the waste places long desolated by war many souls, the trophies of his faithful, personal, ceaseless activity, who, had it not been for his missionary colportage, might have remained in sin, unsought, unwarned, unsaved.

We have thus brought down to the present time the record of this useful man, who, as Army Missionary and as Missionary Colporteur, has written his name and stamped the impress of his soul-loving spirit imperishably upon many hearts.

Following his example and imbibing his spirit, more than forty others-have joined him in this colporteur work of the American Tract Society, to elevate and save the neglected and the lost in that wide portion of our land. No field ever more needed this personal, hand-to-hand and heart-to-heart method of supplying the people with the blessings of education and religion, and on no field have the results been more signal and evident, testifying to the wonderful adaptation of colportage to this emergency.

The situation of the South at the close of the war was truly deplorable. Four years of strife had caused great impoverishment.

Desolation marked the path or the sojourn
of the armies; plantations were devastated,
churches burned, congregations scattered,
and Sabbath-schools broken up. Children
were growing up in ignorance, the prey of
idleness and vice. The sudden emancipa-
tion of a third of the people placed them in
pressing need of sympathy and Christian
instruction. The general impoverishment of
the people rendered the support of the ministry entirely inadequate, and left large districts without stated preaching. Christians
on the field who longed to see their children
taught God's word, were unable to purchase
the requisite elementary books.

Such was the character of the field presented to the American Tract Society, which,
in the Lord's name, entered upon its work of
evangelization. The dearth of religious literature that prevailed, and the religious des-
titutions that everywhere abounded, called
for just such labors.

Something has been done to relieve the
great need; but in the districts remote from
the lines of travel, incessant and highly suc-

cessful labor for two years has scarcely begun the great work to be accomplished. A short time since a colporteur in North Carolina visited in a single week forty-three families, of whom twenty were destitute of the Bible and all religious books. Another in the same state reports a thickly-settled district, where one may travel seventy miles without finding a Sabbath-school. A clergyman in Virginia tells of two whole counties, whose population in 1860 exceeded six thousand, in which there has never been a Sabbath-school.

The colporteurs in their work visit every family in the community, and converse with nearly every individual on personal religion. Sometimes they succeed in organizing a prayer-meeting, and sometimes can induce the people to make provision for the regular preaching of the gospel. But the usual and most successful means of relieving the great destitution is the organization of Sabbath-schools. The children are gathered, and such as are ready to engage in teaching them, whether among the white or colored people, are furnished with books, cards, etc.;

so that all desiring to learn to read the Bible are freely offered the necessary elementary education.

A colporteur in North Carolina, who established schools in several prominent places, says: "The first Sabbath I organized a flourishing school of twenty-four scholars and six teachers; and what is remarkable, not one is a member of any church. On my arrival there, I stated the object of my visit to some, who at once opposed it, saying it was too cold, and no comfortable house could be obtained. I soon found many were disposed to discourage it, which only assured me that God had sent me there to do good.

"So I commenced by asking some little boys if they did not wish to have a school, like other places. They were delighted, and said they would get me a house by morning. Sure enough, on Sabbath morning by sunrise, thirteen children called on me with smiling faces, and informed me that they had a house and a good fire. I soon found my way there, and a crowded house. Several young ladies accompanied me, who said

the boys begged so hard they could not refuse, saying, 'Miss E——, please, madam,
come help us start our school; I know you
can.'

"On arriving at the house, I read a chap-
ter, prayed with them, and lectured the best
I could. I then registered the names of
twenty-four, praying in my heart for God to
also record their names in his book of life;
and such were my feelings, that I found myself in tears in spite of me. Six offered themselves as teachers, and I gave them all, as the
first lesson, the Lord's Prayer and Ten Com-
mandments.

"I called on the teachers a few days ago,
when they informed me the school was increasing, and a doctor was aiding it, saying,
'We are collecting money, and want as large
a library as any school has in the state.' The
merchants said to me, 'We wish now to build
a church and an academy, and we will want
you to get a teacher for us after a while.'

"At G——, I met with a joyful school
when I delivered the libraries there. The
superintendent said, 'Children, save all your

change, and we will get the colporteur to fill our bookcase.' I patiently visited all the houses in the place, and must say that they did all they could, and parted with the last cent. It was court week, and taxes to pay, but nearly every one begged me to call again. I saw ten wagons from the mountains with tobacco and butter. Many of the teamsters I knew, and they were glad to see me, and purchased some books.

"I went next to W——, where I delivered the libraries and books to the teachers, the preacher being absent. It is a flourishing town, noted for its liberality. This place was not molested by either army. The people are happy here, are kind to the freedmen, and give them good wages and homes, and in return are blessed with faithful laborers."

The coöperation of Christians in this work has been encouraging. The whole number of teachers in secular and Sabbath-schools thus provided with the implements of labor, furnished by the Richmond Agency, is about four thousand. The whole number of schools organized, resuscitated, or aided in these two years exceeds one thousand and fifty, with about seventy-five thousand scholars, at an expense of about a third of a dollar to each scholar. Most of these are entirely dependent on this mode of instruction. A friend in North Carolina, acknowledging " a donation of books admirably adapted to our purpose," says: "There are probably more than three thousand children and young persons in this county to whom a door of access is now open, and who will look to and must rely upon colportage, not only for religious but elementary instruction." Similar testimonies might be added from all parts of the field.

Peculiar as is the adaptation of colportage to supplying the wants of the families and neighborhoods and schools of the white population, THE FREEDMEN are even more dependent upon it. Just entering on their new life of freedom, they have displayed an almost insatiable desire to learn to read, and a refreshing readiness to receive the truth of the gospel with a simple, child-like faith. Through the various benevolent agencies of the North, and the self-sacrificing labors of many noble teachers, common schools have been established in most of the *cities and larger villages*. The Freedmen's Bureau reports that one hundred and fifty thousand scholars have been taught in these schools, at a yearly expenditure exceeding $1,200,000, in addition to appropriations made through that Bureau. It is evident that a very small portion of the four millions of freedmen are thus brought under instruction ; nor can the benevolence of the churches support a free school system for the far larger part of this population who reside in the *rural districts*.

How then are they to be furnished with the means of education? If this is to be done, the scholars already taught must engage in the work. Many of them are now employed by the colored people on the plantations, who are so anxious for instruction, that from their scanty resources they contribute cheerfully for their support. The colporteurs of the Society have aided extensively in the organization of these schools in the country, which through want of suitable buildings are

often held under the shade of forest trees or
of brush-arbors, making grants to them of
the Society's elementary books.   Where it
has been impracticable to organize schools,
for want of buildings and teachers, the colporteurs have enlisted members of planters'
families in the work of teaching those in their

employ, and their voluntary aid has been a feature of marked and increasing interest. The progress in this direction has been marvellous. Indifference has passed away, and now the principal obstacle to Sabbath-school instruction among the colored people is *the want of books.* The Society has already distributed two hundred and thirty-four thousand of its "United States Primers;" but what are they among so many?

The spirit of these voluntary teachers is best understood from a few facts connected with their efforts. A colporteur in Virginia writes: "I feel that my labors have not been altogether in vain, having organized a large Sabbath-school for the freedmen at W——. I found one gentleman willing to engage in the work of teaching them, who assured me that he could get the coöperation of some others. As he made an appointment for me, I preached on the second Sabbath to a good congregation, principally of freedmen. They were all interested in the subject, and another gentleman promised to assist in teaching them. Not having suitable books with me, I appointed the fourth Sabbath to organize the school. I was met by a large congregation of freedmen, with some whites. Another gentleman assured me that his heart was in the work, and that the female members of his family would also assist. He at once entered into the organization; and having formerly owned a large number of the freedmen present, knew them and rendered valuable assistance. I was also told that his father would materially aid the enterprise in every way he could. These gentlemen, who took such ready hold of the work, were formerly large slaveholders.

"It was deeply interesting and touching to see the anxiety to learn that was manifested by the negroes. Gray-headed old men were there, and gave their names as scholars wanting to learn to read. There were those from near eighty years of age down to ten, or perhaps younger, evincing the greatest satisfaction and pleasure at the prospect. One man said to me that he did not expect to learn much himself, but he wanted his children to be taught. I am deeply interested in this work, and believe that Christians have a large and inviting field of usefulness open before them in this direction. I rejoice that so many of the most influential of our citizens are lending their influence to the work of educating the blacks."

A young lady of fine literary attainments, bearing a name eminent in the annals of Virginia, endeavored to establish a school among the freedmen in the neighborhood of her mother's plantation. After writing to the various sources for books without success, and vainly endeavoring to persuade the neighbors to allow her to use one of their barns for a schoolroom, she finally established her school on the side of the road under a few old oaks, near an old blacksmith's shop, the scholars being seated on some rough planks. The teachers who aided her were five schoolboys and two little girls of seven and nine. She then wrote to the Society's agency at Richmond for books, which were promptly forwarded to her from funds given by a Sabbath-school in New England. In acknowledging their reception,

she says, "Until last Sabbath, when your
First Lessons and Primers were distributed
to a happy crowd, we averaged two books,
generally different in kind, to a class. I have
the A-B-C department, and have had but one
book to sometimes over thirty scholars; so

we made a blackboard of the sandy road before us, in which we traced the letters, and
twenty of my class have learned their letters,

large and small, in the sand, and on manuscript cards which they had taken home."

In a letter from this lady asking for more books, she says : "All my books are exhausted now, and a number of new scholars are unsupplied, although I have used all the Tract Primers which were to have been reserved for prizes for the highest attainments. I wish the children who sent the books could see the crowd pressing up and begging for them, as if they were begging for bread: 'Give me one.' 'Give me a book.' 'Oh, please give me one.' 'You promise *me* one las' time,' etc. Yesterday I noticed among the new-comers a very bright boy, about eight years old, who watched the distribution of the books with intense interest. Just as the last were given out of the basket, I asked him if he had a book. The little fellow burst into a bitter cry, and hiding his face in his sister's apron, sobbed out, 'You never give me none.' Fortunately I found a picture-alphabet book, which soon dried the tears on little Joe's cheeks, and sent him home happier than ever before in his life."

She continued her school by the wayside until near Christmas, when it became so cold that she was unable longer to teach in that place. Mr. H. E. Simmons, one of the Society's agents in New England, having become acquainted with the history of this interesting school, was able, through the benevolence of a gentleman in Boston, to furnish her the means of building a log schoolhouse, which he presented to her in person at her home in Virginia.

A Virginia pastor, after successfully conducting Sabbath-schools for the freedmen within his parish during the summer, was unwilling that instruction should cease when the schools closed for the winter. By systematic and persevering effort he organized a school in nearly every family, taught by the white members of his churches; and thus the work so prospered, that the short winter was found even more favorable in its results than the long summer.

From every portion of the field assurances come that the best Sabbath-school teachers in the churches are either already engaged

in this work, or can be secured. Nothing is
wanting greatly to increase the number of
those ready to devote themselves to the service of the Lord in this direction *without pay*,
but the means to furnish them with the
books required, which they in their poverty
are unable to buy. Will not the friends of
the Tract Society who can appreciate the
importance and the wide extent of the work
that can thus be done for Christ, cheerfully
furnish the Society with means, so that all
willing to engage in this benevolent work
may be supplied with the facilities for carry-
ing it successfully forward?

We might give many illustrations of the
good realized from the donations of individuals or Sabbath-schools, as they have been
furnished to needy schools, or to those voluntary laborers, to aid them in their good
work. The following incident, related by
by Uncle John, shows the far-reaching influence of a small donation of fifteen dollars
intrusted to his care.

In midsummer of 1865, travelling south-
ward from Richmond, he left the train at

C—— station, bearing upon his shoulder a heavy package of books. He was not long in learning that a large number of freedmen, employed in the coal mines near at hand, were without a school, and that no one was caring for their spiritual wants. Continuing his visitation and inquiries, he met, three miles distant, a planter ready to devote his Sabbaths to the religious education of the negroes. He also found a convenient building, circulated an appointment, and on the next Lord's day met over one hundred scholars. Immediate use was made of the contents of the package, from which Uncle John presented spellers, primers, and a card large enough to be seen by all in the house. He gave them their first lesson in concert. It was laying the foundation of a mighty work. A few months later, the colored people, not content with Sabbath-school instruction, hired a godly brother of their own race to teach their children during the week. The Spirit wrought through him; many souls were converted, a church was organized, and the teacher has become an ordained minister."

At a subsequent visit Uncle John was much encouraged by the progress of the school, and wrote : "Many of the colored people of that vicinity evince much talent ; most of the children can read, some write, and one class is doing well in arithmetic. Several girls will soon be able to go out and teach; so we hope to furnish help for other places next year. The best of all is, that many are seeking the Lord. One hundred souls have recently professed to give their hearts to Jesus. I feel thankful that I was ever permitted to visit that place. I wish the friends that gave the fifteen dollars' worth of books that started that school, could see the progress made by the children. They surely would praise God, as we did yesterday in visiting the place."

What a blessing upon so small a gift to the Lord. Were ever fifteen dollars invested which brought greater gain? Over one hundred children educated; several teachers fitted for blessing others; but above all, one hundred precious souls saved from death to enjoy God for ever; and a church already organized for the edification of these believers, and the salvation of other deathless spirits.

An English mother, who has been thirty years in Canada, sent seven dollars for the freedmen, through the Rochester Agency of the American Tract Society, desiring to hear of the manner of its appropriation. It was given to a colporteur in North Carolina, who sent the following account of its disposition:

"I have not given it to a colored Sabbath-school, from the fact that our Sabbath-schools among the freedmen cannot be carried on in the winter for the want of suitable houses. In the warm season, their schools were conducted in the open air, in a grove, and some under a brush-arbor. The same is also the case with some white Sabbath-schools. I have made use of the lady's charity, however, in a different, and I hope more profitable manner. I have visited the poor negroes in their own cabins and around their firesides. I have sat and taught them, parents and children, to spell and read, and have freely given them Primers and Testaments; and when they would commence giving me many thanks, I have told them that they were not indebted to me, but, under God, to a lady in Canada who wished them well. Their astonishment was great. With tears of gratitude in their eyes they have said, 'God bless the lady, and God bless the Tract Society, and God bless you.'

"On one occasion, when I gave Primers and First Lessons to some children, and told them who was their benefactress, the mother expressed an anxious desire to see the lady, that she might thank her for her kindness. I told her that it was not probable she could ever see her in this life, but if she would be a faithful Christian here, she would no doubt be permitted to meet the good lady in heaven, where there would be no distinction of color, but all would be alike transformed into the glorious image of our blessed Saviour. At this idea a shout of rapturous joy burst from the lips of the old colored woman. The colporteur caught the spirit of universal love. We all knelt in prayer, and drank copiously of the fountain that flows from the throne of God."

A lad of twelve years, a member of a Sabbath-school in Buffalo, N. Y., made a donation of twenty dollars, his missionary money, to be used at the South through the Richmond Agency of the Tract Society. It was used for the organization and aid of *four Sabbath-schools* in the vicinity of Raleigh, N. C., and was expended for books. Before twelve months had elapsed, many of the scholars in these schools had learned to read, and from twelve to fifteen souls had obtained a saving knowledge of Christ, and were laboring for the instruction and salvation of others. Surely in the last day these redeemed souls will rise up to call that child "blessed" who was thus the means of giving them a knowledge of Christ and his love. Will not many others make use of the same instrumentality for doing good, thus extending the privileges they enjoy to many of the ignorant and neglected, and blessing many homes with light, knowledge, and salvation during their lives, and meeting at last the welcome plaudit,

"Inasmuch as ye have done it to one of the least of these my brethren, ye have done it unto me?"

The crowning feature of the whole is the manifest token of God's presence and approval in the conversion of souls. The first book uniformly desired by those who have newly learned to read is the New Testament. Revivals have been in progress in many of the schools that have been founded, and in several places churches have arisen in less than a year after the organization of the school. No record has been kept of the number of those who have been led to Christ by the colporteurs, or in the schools they have formed or aided. Their record is on high; and in the last great day, when the books are opened, it shall be said of many, "This man was born there."

Such is a brief sketch of the work which the benevolence of Northern Christians has enabled the American Tract Society to accomplish in the South. The work has barely commenced. But two years have elapsed

since the first colporteur began his Christian
visitations, and already with gratitude we are
compelled to say, "What has God wrought!"
What may we not hope for, if, through the
continued benevolence and enlarged liberality of those who bid Godspeed to the work,
the agencies for extending it are greatly in-
creased, and the stores of educational and
religious literature prepared by the Society
are widely diffused where they are so urgent-
ly needed?

The work commends itself to the heart of
every patriot, philanthropist, and Christian.
The evils to be removed are immense and
appalling; the system here presented is simple and effective. When it was explained in
a public meeting in Washington, and the
results it had already accomplished were
reported, Hon. Frederick T. Frelinghuysen,
United States Senator from New Jersey, in
an eloquent address claimed that these earnest laborers in the Tract Society had caught,
as by inspiration, the one great need of the
nation. Their evangelizing efforts must be
effective in allaying strife and promoting

peace and good-will between the different sections of the land. He would have colporteurs sent into every county. He would have every Sabbath-school in the North sustain from one to six Sabbath-schools in the South, and would have these laborers and their cause liberally supported.

Hon. Henry Wilson, United States Senator from Massachusetts, followed him, warmly commending the design and purposes of the Tract Society, and the excellent adaptation of its means to the end to be accomplished. He greatly valued these truly Christian influences for settling our national difficulties. Turning to members of Congress many of whom were present, he said with emphasis, "*These men and this agency are doing more for reconstruction than all of us.*" He endorsed the wish of Senator Frelinghuysen, that the Sabbath-schools North would, through the Society, send down their means by thousands for founding Sabbath-schools all over the South.

We trust that the generous sympathies of the members of Northern churches and Sab-

bath-schools may respond to this desire of
these eminent statesmen, elicited by the con-
vincing evidence presented to them, that God
has called the American Tract Society to
occupy the vast and needy field at the South.
With a system of lay effort which can reach
every family; with the coöperation of resi-
dent Christians of every class in the work of
Sabbath-school instruction; with a literature
full of Christ, and suited to the wants of the
people, and a depository in the needy district; and with the blessing of God's Spirit
leading hundreds and thousands by this
means to salvation, we have every encouragement to carry out the spirit of the resolution adopted at the anniversary at the close
of the war, "in Christ's name to strive, with
all good men, to make the desolated South a
garden of the Lord."

DESCRIPTION

OF

THE TRACT HOUSE.

The following appreciative notice of the Society's house and work, appeared August 21st, in the *New York Evening Gazette,* edited by CHARLES H. SWEETSER. It contains information of interest to the friends of the Society.

OF the multitudinous societies established by Christian charity, and for civilizing and Christianizing purposes, we believe the two that rank the highest for the thorough system with which their affairs are managed, are the American Bible Society and American Tract Society. With both these organizations our readers are in a good measure familiar, so far as their general field and results are concerned. Very few, however, understand how great is the machinery, and how extensive are the practical details attendant upon the working of these two great institutions. At some future time we propose to give an extended description of the Bible Society, and its practical working. Our present sketch will have to do with the Tract Society only, to chronicle the various facts, concerning which we have taken note-book in hand, and passed through the entire establishment.

A GLANCE BACKWARD.

This national institution was organized forty-two years ago, the other tract societies then existing becoming auxiliary to it, and is the same to-day in its plan and purpose that it was at the start. At the time of its founding, the receipts of all the tract societies in the country did not exceed $20,000 per annum. Last year the receipts of the American Tract Society were over five hundred thousand dollars! The offices of the Society have always been in this city, and where the Society's building now stands.

THE BUILDING.

The building owned and occupied by the Society, is located at 150 Nassau-street, just opposite the *Times* building. It was erected in 1825, the year the Society was formed, by funds contributed in New York;

and rebuilt and enlarged in 1846 by a loan secured by mortgage on the premises, to be paid from proceeds of rents of parts of the building not occupied by the Society. It is eighty feet by ninety-four, and five stories high, besides basement for storing paper, and sub-cellar for coal. The first floor is occupied by the Society's general depository, sales-room, treasurer's office, and stores; the second furnishes rooms for the American Messenger and Child's Paper, and other offices; the third contains the Committee-room, executive offices, and composing-room; the fourth is the bindery, and the fifth the press-room. The printing and hydraulic presses, and other machinery, are propelled, and the entire building is also heated by steam. The central court is excavated, and forms a boiler-room.

THE MEN WHO DO THE WORK.

The working force in the House consists of a Secretary and Assistant in each department.

Of the *Publishing Department*, Rev. Wm. A. Hallock is Secretary. He is the founder of the Society, has watched over all its interests with incessant care, and has been its most prominent officer, holding the most responsible position in it, as editor of all its issues. He is a man of singleness of purpose, strength of will, and an unswerving adherence to what he considers right. Few men have performed as many years of unceasing labor as he, and with such widespread and beneficent results.

Rev. W. W. Rand, his Assistant, is the scholar, the practical editor of the Foreign as well as the English publications; and the musical critic, composer, and compiler of the Society's hymn-books. The Bible Dictionary and Happy Voices were prepared by him.

In the Financial Department, Rev. O. Eastman is Secretary, and O. R. Kingsbury, Assistant Secretary and Acting Treasurer. They have been connected with the Society from the second or third year of its existence. They are laborious, painstaking, rigidly economical, and of sound judgment. To them, under the supervision of the Financial Committee, the public are chiefly indebted for the wise and uniformly safe management of the pecuniary interests of the institution.

In the Colportage and General Distribution Department, Rev. John M. Stevenson is Secretary, and S. E. Warner, Assistant. They are occupied in securing and supervising colporteurs, examining, and, with the Distributing Committee, deciding upon unnumbered requests for grants, preparing articles for the periodicals, and attending to the details of a multifarious and world-wide correspondence.

W. B. Bodge and J. W. Brown have charge of the printing department, and Mr. Foot of the binding. Their skill and taste are seen in the style of the publications of the Society.

S. W. Stebbins is General Depositary, and forwards the publications to all the agencies.

WHAT IS DONE.

Four thousand bound volumes, pamphlets, tracts, and papers are turned out by the Society every working-day of the year. In July last the total number of volumes received at the depository from the various departments, exclusive of tracts, etc., was ninety-nine thousand seven hundred and sixty-two. Of the little Sabbath-school hymn-book known as *Happy Voices*, 246,000 copies have been published. Of the *Bible Dictionary*, 124,000 copies. Of the *Christian Almanac*, 120,000 copies are printed annually. Of the *American Messenger*, there are printed 163,000 copies monthly; of the *German Messenger*, 32,000 copies; and of the *Child's Paper*, 353,000 copies. The Society has published, during its existence, 22,000,000 volumes! This will give some idea of the vast amount of work done at the printing-house of the Society.

THE COMPOSING ROOM.

In the composing room there are nine compositors, of whom one is employed entirely on German, and one on Spanish, French, and other foreign languages. There is one proof-reader, one female to read copy, and one man employed in repairing stereotype plates. All works are either stereotyped or electrotyped, except the *German Messenger* and *Annual Report*.

In the composing room some fifteen languages are set, and the music for the publications of the Society is also set here. Mr. Bodge has had charge of this department for twenty-one years, and conducts it with great care and success.

THE ENGRAVING DEPARTMENT.

Here are produced all the illustrations used in the publications of the Society. Seven engravers are kept constantly employed, and many others a portion of their time, in preparing new pictures on wood or steel for the numerous books, tracts, etc., issuing from the presses of the Society, prominent among which is that favorite of Sunday-school children—and older heads too—*The Child's Paper.*

The designs are made by the best artists in the country, and paid for liberally. The Society has on hand a large accumulation of beautiful engravings, amounting to several thousand, which they are continually using in the reproduction of their books, papers, etc.

It may be said here that the Society many years ago resolved to illustrate their cheap books in as handsome a manner as they could by first-class designing, engraving, and printing. That they succeeded in outstripping all others is well known ; and the fact that the poorest in the land have been able to purchase a book—no matter how small the size or price—whose pictures, whether many or few, would compare with the very finest illustrated works produced in this country, has had no small influence in educating the taste of the people and creating a desire for finely illustrated books, thus giving a higher standard and impetus to the book-trade greater than is generally acknowledged. This department is skilfully conducted by Mr. Elias J. Whitney.

THE PRESS ROOM.

There are employed in the press and sheet room fifty-eight persons—forty-two males and sixteen females. There are eighteen Adams presses, two cylinder presses, and one hand press. Mr. John W. Brown is foreman in this department, and has been for twenty-one years.

THE DRYING ROOM.

This is an important adjunct to the establishment. Here all the sheets are dried before they pass to the bindery. There are four hydraulic presses in this room.

FOLDING ROOM.

It is no small matter to fold all the sheets that go into four thousand issues daily. Seven are employed constantly in folding papers, and sixty are engaged in folding the sheets of books.

THE BINDERY.

There are employed in the bindery ninety-five girls and forty-three men. A book passes through many hands before it is ready for delivery at the depository. Mr. Andrew Foot is superintendent of the bindery, and is introducing improvements which cannot fail to make the work of this department still more acceptable.

HOW THE WORK IS DONE.

The printing done by the Tract Society is not surpassed in the world. Mr. Baker, of Baker & Godwin, the well-known printers, testified to this after a tour among the foreign printing houses. He said : "I think it safe to say there is no secret known to the European printers which we are not in possession of. Perhaps I may be mistaken ; but I believe we can duplicate the most sumptuous work of the English, French, or German press.

"And in this connection I cannot forbear speaking of the rapid advancement which has been made, comparatively recently, in printing here, growing out of the increasing demand for better and more expensive books. Perhaps no press has done more than the Tract House to develop this taste ; and I have often expressed my gratification that an opportunity was afforded this Society to exhibit the capacity of our workmen to develop the beautiful in our art. I am sure the objects of this Society have not been perverted in thus elevating the tastes of the people, and also indirectly softening the hearts of the publishers, who, if not mentioned in the Society's preamble as subjects of their mission, have yet, fortunately, been reached by the tract printer's excellence."

MAILING DEPARTMENT.

Five persons are engaged all the time in mailing the *Child's Paper* and *Messenger*. Mr. Thomas M. Lawrence has had charge of this department for twenty-five years.

THE DEPOSITORY.

The depository and store on the first floor is in charge of Mr. S. W. Stebbins. The sales at the store amount to about $50,000 per annum, aside from the general work of the Society.

CORRESPONDENCE.

The correspondence of the Society is very large. About ten thousand letters are received every year. All the letters are preserved, and have been since the founding of the Society. They are bound up in 150 volumes, containing 1,000 letters each, all ready for reference.

UNION BASIS.

The publications of the Society are all based upon the truths and duties generally received by evangelical Christians. The Publishing Committee is composed of Presbyterian, Congregational, Baptist, Episcopalian, and Dutch Reformed, and without the assent of all no book is issued. The book department supports itself.

BENEVOLENT DEPARTMENT.

The donations given to the Society last year amounted to $160,000, which was expended, except what was given to increase the stock of publications, in three ways :

I. Cash to foreign missionary boards.

II. By grants of books and tracts to seamen, soldiers, chaplains, literary institutions, humane institutions, mission Sabbath-schools, missionaries, and to individuals to do good with. About one third of the benevolent receipts of the Society are thus spent yearly. Since the Society began, forty-two years ago, $1,120,000 have been spent in this way.

III. By colporteurs—men who combine with the circulation of Bibles, books, and tracts by sale and gift in the destitute parts of the land, religious conversation, prayer, formation of Sabbath-schools, promotion of temperance, etc.

Colportage originated in 1841. Colporteurs of the Society have performed 4,000 years of labor, circulated 11,000,000 volumes, and made 9,600,000 family visits. Grand results. There are at present one hundred and sixty colporteurs. Perhaps one half of the benevolent funds of the Society are expended annually in this way.

www.ingramcontent.com/pod-product-compliance
Lightning Source LLC
Chambersburg PA
CBHW032249080426
42735CB00008B/1060